SARAH BURGESS

Sarah Burgess is a New York-based playwright from Alexandria, Virginia. Her plays include *Kings* (Public Theater, New York). *Dry Powder* received the Laurents/Hatcher Foundation Award and was a finalist for the Susan Smith Blackburn Prize.

Other Titles in this Series

Sarah Burgess

DRY POWDER

NICK HERN BOOKS

London

www.nickhernbooks.co.uk

A Nick Hern Book

Dry Powder first published in Great Britain as a paperback original in 2018 by Nick Hern Books Limited, The Glasshouse, 49a Goldhawk Road, London W12 8QP

Cover artwork: SWD; photography: Shaun Webb

Designed and typeset by Nick Hern Books, London
Printed in the UK by Mimeo Ltd, Huntingdon, Cambridgeshire PE29 6XX

A CIP catalogue record for this book is available from the British Library

ISBN 978 1 84842 728 0

Dry Powder received its world premiere at the Public Theater, New York (Oskar Eustis, Artistic Director; Patrick Willingham, Executive Director), on 1 March 2016. The cast was as follows:

RICK	Hank Azaria
JENNY	Claire Danes
SETH	John Krasinski
JEFF SHRADER	Sanjit De Silva

Director	Thomas Kail
Scenic Designer	Rachel Hauck
Costume Designer	Clint Ramos
Lighting Designer	Jason Lyons
Original Music and Sound Designer	Lindsay Jones

The play received its UK premiere at Hampstead Theatre, London, on 1 February 2018 (previews from 26 January). The cast was as follows:

RICK	Aidan McArdle
JENNY	Hayley Atwell
SETH	Tom Riley
JEFF SHRADER	Joseph Balderrama

Director	Anna Ledwich
Designer	Andrew D Edwards
Lighting Designer	Elliot Griggs
Sound Designer	Max Pappenheim
Video Designer	Ian William Galloway

Characters

RICK, *forty-five to sixty;*
 Founder and President, KMM Capital Management

JENNY, *thirty to forty;*
 Founding Director, KMM Capital Management

SETH, *Seth is exactly Jenny's age;*
 Founding Director, KMM Capital Management

JEFF SCHRADER, *thirty-five to forty-five;*
 CEO, Landmark Luggage

Notes

Slashes (/) or (//) indicate where the next line should begin.

This text went to press before the end of rehearsals and so may differ slightly from the play as performed.

1.

Friday.

KMM Capital Management. Midtown Manhattan.

RICK *reads something on his phone.*

JENNY *enters* RICK*'s office.*

JENNY. You wanted to see me?

RICK. Yes.

JENNY. Is this about Landmark Luggage? I saw you stop into Seth's meeting. I have some thoughts on that.

RICK. Are you speaking to a finance class at NYU?

JENNY. Oh. Yes. In two weeks.

RICK. Why are you speaking to a finance class at NYU?

JENNY. Remember that consultant we brought in on American Saddle? Baljeet Nair? Orthopedic shoe, skin issues.

RICK. No.

JENNY. He teaches finance undergrads at NYU now. He asked me to come in and speak to them.

RICK. About what?

JENNY. He said to talk about whatever I want.

RICK. You will not say whatever you want.

JENNY. Why not?

RICK. What are you planning to say?

JENNY. I only have a rough draft at this stage.

RICK. Let me hear it please.

JENNY. What?

RICK. Please let me hear what you're going to say to a roomful of college kids with video-recording devices while I am getting eviscerated daily because of this goddamn layoff announcement.

JENNY. Oh. Wait are you serious?

RICK. Yes Jenny.

JENNY. Why would we do that with our time?

RICK. Because they're going after our LPs now – that's all of our investors.

JENNY. Of course they're protesting, that's what unemployed people do.

RICK. Well they're doing it outside the Beckwith office today. Howard just had his coffee slapped out of his hand.

JENNY. They're just a bunch of socialists and whack-jobs.

RICK. The media isn't portraying them as whack-jobs.

JENNY. Of course not.

RICK. The media is portraying me as an unprecedented asshole.

JENNY. But who takes *The New York Times* seriously?

RICK. The Earth. The entire Earth.

JENNY. I meant: who in our world.

RICK. They were outside the Snyder office too. Did you know that? Gene's car got surrounded.

JENNY. Is he okay?

RICK. I talked to Gene, he's fine. It's very clever, harassing our LPs like this – they're going right after our money. It's a good thing the Gjertsons are based in Oslo.

JENNY. Our past two funds were top quartile. Legitimately top quartile. Our LPs aren't going to abandon us because some jealous reporters made fun of your party elephants.

RICK. Elephant. There was just one.

JENNY. Thought I saw two.

RICK. Why does everyone think there were two?

JENNY. Were there mirrors in the ballroom?

RICK. Fucking elephant. I should've talked her out of it. She had to have an engagement party that tied thematically to the wedding.

JENNY. There'll be elephants at your wedding?

RICK. No just because it's in Bali.

JENNY. There are elephants in Bali?

RICK. Yes Jenny. I have a home there. I engage in philanthropy there.

JENNY. Okay.

RICK. I should have cancelled the goddamn party.

JENNY. Yeah. Successful people don't deserve engagement parties. We should all just move to caves.

RICK. It is painfully obvious that you don't understand how serious this is.

JENNY. No, I understand. I'm sure the protests are annoying our LPs, and I'm sure *The Times* article was upsetting for Katie.

RICK. Yes.

JENNY. But you've worked seventy hours a week for thirty years. You've earned every cent of your wealth. You're allowed to have any kind of party you want.

RICK. That's not the issue, Jenny. The issue was having the party on the exact day of the layoff announcement.

JENNY. The layoffs were inevitable. It's not your fault ShopGreat allowed itself to be commandeered by unions.

RICK. That is also not the issue. This is about timing and perception. And boy, do you not have talent in either of those areas.

JENNY. It's not a lack of talent. It's being rational. I don't waste time trying to prevent outcomes I can't change.

RICK. I could have changed the outcome.

JENNY. How?

RICK. I could have listened to Seth. He told me to cancel the party. But you advised me not to. Which is hilarious, because you don't even enjoy parties.

JENNY. Sure I do.

RICK. No you don't.

JENNY. It was very fun.

RICK. I don't want to hear any more about the party.

JENNY. I apologize.

RICK. And on top of this unbelievable nightmare, Xu Wei called again.

JENNY. He did?

RICK. Wanted us to fly to Hong Kong. Can you imagine if that got out in the press?

JENNY. How much?

RICK. He wanted to commit fifty-five million. I told him the fund's closed.

JENNY. I mean fifty-five million's / fifty-five million.

RICK. / I said Wei, do not call here again. You are an international joke. And particularly right now, I do not need to be doing business with a corrupt asshole like you.

JENNY. Oh, wow, you said that?

RICK. I wasn't quite that polite.

JENNY. Was he upset?

RICK. I don't want him calling anymore.

JENNY. I heard Lakeshire's taking a commitment from him.

RICK. Of course they are. They're classless. Everyone knows where his money comes from.

JENNY. Can we talk about Landmark Luggage? What's the price?

RICK. We will talk about that later.

JENNY. I bet it's seven-hundred million at least. I had one of my analysts take one of Seth's analysts out for bibimbap so he could pump him for data on Landmark's assets. Did you know Landmark owns a jet and huge building in downtown Sacramento?

RICK. So it'll be easier to raise debt.

JENNY. Okay but even if it's highly leveraged, I'm not seeing this as worthwhile.

RICK. It looks like an intriguing opportunity. You know how good Seth is at finding unique deals.

JENNY. I don't know that that's how I'd put it.

RICK. Oh you don't? How about this? When it comes to bringing me targets, he's about a thousand times more effective than you are. Now tell me what you're going to say at NYU.

JENNY. My notes are in my office.

RICK. Then go get them.

She goes.

RICK *dials someone on his phone.*

(*On phone.*) Sam did you hear back from *The Times*?

…

Did you not tell me yesterday that you had contacts there?

…

I don't care, do your job.

He hangs up. JENNY *returns.*

JENNY. You want just bullet points or…

RICK. I want you to read the whole thing.

JENNY. It's not a cohesive unit yet.

RICK. Just read it.

JENNY. Okay. So. Out there, that's the class. You're like one of the students. Okay.

She reads from her notes.

I want to first extend a thank-you to Professor Nair for having me come talk to you guys today. So great to see your shining faces.

Professor Nair says this class is mostly Seniors. That means this May you enter the real world.

(*To* RICK.) And then I'll say something like welcoming them to the real world.

RICK. Okay.

JENNY. So then I'll segue to the wisdom I want to share with them.

RICK. You don't need to explain what you're doing.

JENNY. Okay.

(*Delivering her speech.*) You guys are finance majors. That tells me you're prudent. Let me give you some advice about the life you have chosen. As you probably know, I'm a founding director at KMM Capital Management. Our firm was in the news recently. / Because we

RICK. / Our firm is currently in the news, one.

JENNY. This is two weeks away, so I'm projecting into the future.

RICK. And two: Don't bring that up.

JENNY. It ties into my point. I want to / talk about

RICK. / Okay, okay just keep going, keep going.

JENNY. Well now I've lost my train of thought.

RICK. This is trying my fucking patience.

JENNY. You wanted to hear what I had so far.

RICK. Yeah. Sometime today please.

JENNY. I apologize.

She finds her place.

Oh, okay.

Our firm was in the news recently. Because we had the audacity to perform our function.

Not that it's surprising. It's an Us versus Them situation right now.

Ever notice, when one of us splurges on a party at a cost of say, five percent of our annual income, it's shameful. But when one of them splurges on a party at that *same relative cost*, it's fun.

RICK. You will not say that.

JENNY. Okay I'll cut that. Yeah it's a rough draft.

RICK. Go on.

JENNY. Ever notice, when we get together in a private meeting among peers, it's an evil cabal. But when they get together in a private meeting among peers, it's a labor union.

RICK. No.

JENNY. Okay I'll cut that.

(*The speech*.) You guys need to know: The game is rigged against us. Why? Because they want what we have. And you have to admit, it's a good strategy, vilifying the successful. If you want to steal, first you find a mark. Now you discredit your mark. You stoke popular resentment, until that resentment turns to hate. You discredit your mark. That is how you steal.

(*To* RICK.) Then I'll ask them: 'Does that sound extreme?' And when they're nodding I'll say:

It's not extreme. It's the truth.

When you graduate in May, you go to war.

RICK. I forbid you from saying that.

JENNY. I'll cut war. Here's the ending.

RICK. (*A sound*.)

JENNY. I have few core beliefs. I'll leave you with one:

Nobody is saying free enterprise is perfect. Sometimes it isn't very nice, especially to the weak. But, free enterprise is fair. It asks nothing of you but that you show up and join the competition. That's not imperialistic, that's not corrupt, that's not racist, that's not sexist. That's beautiful.

A pause.

That's all I have so far.

He's not happy.

Thoughts?

RICK. Just one. You're not saying any of that.

JENNY. Any of it?

RICK. Any of it.

JENNY. Rick, this is two weeks away. Everything will have blown over by then.

RICK. Throw all of that out. Just give them an overview of what you do.

JENNY. Everything I do is confidential.

RICK. Walk through the fundamentals of private equity.

JENNY. They're finance majors, they already know the fundamentals of private equity.

RICK. Then tell some nice stories from your life, things people can relate to.

JENNY. People can't relate to me.

RICK. Okay. I'm about to fucking lose it.

JENNY. I apologize.

RICK. You said they're finance majors. They're probably exactly like you were in college.

JENNY. I didn't go to NYU.

RICK. Pleasing anecdotes. Enough to fill fifteen minutes.

JENNY. Okay.

RICK. 'Hi. I'm Rick. I'm the founder and president of KMM. I used to do M&A at Goldman.'

JENNY. Okay yeah.

RICK. 'I'm from Maryland. I like the Orioles. Any O's fans in the house?'

JENNY. Any what in the house?

RICK. O's fans.

JENNY. What?

RICK. O's fans.

JENNY. I'm not getting it.

RICK. O's fans. The Baltimore Orioles.

JENNY. Oh. Yes, I understand.

RICK. Just don't say anything that people will criticize.

JENNY. People will criticize anything.

RICK. Jenny. Just say something inoffensive for fifteen minutes. Jesus fucking Christ.

JENNY. Okay, alright. I'll do something else. I'll run it by Sam in PR.

RICK. No you'll run it by me.

She starts to reply.

Out.

Lights.

2.

Monday.

KMM Capital Management.

JENNY, RICK, SETH.

SETH. Are you alright?

RICK. Yes.

JENNY. Haven't been sleeping?

SETH. Are the LPs upset?

RICK. It's fine.

SETH. How are the folks at the Beckwith Trust?

RICK. Let's talk about this deal please. Do I do this or not?

JENNY. No.

RICK. Seth?

SETH. Yes.

RICK. Why?

SETH. Rick, I'm gonna be brutally honest right now. This week has been the lowest point in the history of our firm. But Landmark is about to solve all our problems. This deal will return roughly three times our invested capital, / and it will

JENNY. / What do you mean by 'roughly'?

SETH. Two-point-eight to three-point-two. And it will completely change the narrative on us right now. The media will stop trashing you. The protests will stop.

RICK. Explain.

SETH. Jeff Schrader and I have come up with an exciting new business model that will increase revenue and create jobs at the same time.

RICK. What's the price?

SETH. Glad you asked. Yesterday talking to Jeff Schrader, I said let's do this, what's a number that'll satisfy Stu? And you know what we arrived at?

JENNY. Seven hundred million.

SETH. No.

JENNY. More than seven hundred?

SETH. No.

JENNY. More than *eight*? More than eight hundred. We're not doing this deal.

SETH. No. Four-nine-one.

RICK. What?

SETH. Yeah.

JENNY. That can't be right.

RICK. Why would they do that?

SETH. They want us to be the buyer. And I got them down from five-seven-five.

RICK. Jesus that's a good price.

SETH. Stu's ready to do this – he wants to retire.

RICK. Stu?

SETH. The owner.

     It's hard to source deals these days, Rick. This is a no-brainer.

RICK. Jenny, four-nine-one.

JENNY. No yeah it's a good price.

RICK. What about financing?

SETH. Looks like we can do it with only twenty percent.

RICK. Get out of here.

SETH. That'd be our lowest equity position in what, three years?

JENNY. The banks won't accept eighty percent debt-to-cap.

SETH. I've already lined it up. The bank will do three hundred and my buddy at Prism Capital said they'll provide the rest for sure.

RICK. Impressive.

SETH. Thank you.

JENNY. Hold on, does Landmark understand that this is a leveraged buyout?

SETH. Of course they do.

JENNY. They know this deal will load them up with debt.

SETH. 'Load them up' is a bit extreme. But yes of course they know this will involve debt.

(*To* RICK.) At eighty percent leverage, this is a slam dunk.

RICK. Four-nine-one at twenty percent equity.

SETH. That's only ninety-eight-point-two out of the remaining dry powder.

JENNY. Rick, the numbers are fine.

RICK. You thought it'd be seven hundred.

JENNY. Yes. It's a good price.

RICK. You were way off.

SETH. The fund has what, three hundred and seventy million left to invest?

RICK. Yes.

JENNY. So, sure, ninety-eight-point-two is potentially acceptable but if there's / no exit

RICK. / Hold on, are they hiring a sell-side banker?

SETH. No.

RICK. They could try to start an auction.

SETH. They won't. It's just us and them. Stu listens to Jeff Schrader, and Jeff Schrader wants to run this new disruptive iteration of Landmark.

JENNY. Are you giving a TED talk?

RICK. Shh.

SETH. And no other PE shops are even looking at them. We can get it for four-nine-one.

RICK. Jenny. It's dramatically underpriced, it's a skinny equity check. Seth has a plan. This looks very attractive.

JENNY. Sure, no I see that boss. One question, what's the exit?

SETH. We could sell to a strategic buyer, but I honestly think this could be an IPO.

JENNY. You always think your companies will go public.

SETH. I don't.

JENNY. You do.

SETH. My and Jeff's new online business model will drive growth from four hundred million net sales to anywhere from six-fifty to seven-fifty in a few short years. This could be huge.

RICK (*to* JENNY). We have an exit concept. We have a projected return multiple of at least what?

SETH. At least two-point-eight. We'll almost certainly triple our money.

RICK. So what's the problem?

JENNY. Seth himself admits that no one else is interested in Landmark. If no one else is considering this deal, then what I might ask, Rick, is why is that? And there are two possible answers to that question. One, Seth correctly sees value here that's invisible to everybody else, and is therefore a genius. Or two: every other PE shop has correctly concluded that this would be a stupid investment.

SETH. Why should we do this when no one else is biting right now? Because that's having vision.

JENNY. Oh gosh, so you're saying it's the first option. You're saying you're a genius.

SETH. Your words. Jeff's really looking forward to our meeting on Thursday.

JENNY. He's flying out already?

SETH. We're at that stage. We have a finalized Letter of Intent.

JENNY. Are you sending our jet?

SETH. Of course not. Landmark's flying him out.

JENNY. Commercial?

SETH. No. Landmark has a Citation Ten.

JENNY. Right. So, this CEO, your guy Jeff, would you say he spends money recklessly or he spends money foolishly?

SETH. Okay, Jeff didn't want it. Apparently Stu always dreamed about owning a corporate jet. They finally pulled the trigger a few years ago. But they do charter it out when they aren't using it.

JENNY. Oh, so Landmark is also an airline. Great. The luggage and the plane.

RICK. It's fine. We'll deal with that later. The meeting is on Thursday? When?

SETH. Ten. My assistant coordinated with your assistants.

RICK. Jenny, I haven't heard anything from you that makes this a No.

JENNY. Seth wants to grow Landmark into the online Samsonite. Who's asking for an online Samsonite?

SETH. Rick, disintermediation will kill two birds. One, it'll make way for a more modern distribution structure, and two, it'll cut costs. Plus Jeff Schrader has the potential to be an honest-to-god superstar. With a few changes, they have serious growth potential.

RICK. So why are they selling?

JENNY. Exactly. Why are they selling?

SETH. Stu is selling because he's seventy-nine. He needs to cash out. That's all.

RICK. Sounds pretty fucking ideal.

SETH. I knew you'd like it.

JENNY. Okay. Rick, I've been recalibrating now that I know the price is four-nine-one. So I'll tell you what would make this deal worthwhile – we do buy Landmark. Then we stop production –

SETH. No.

JENNY. We initiate zero-based budgeting –

SETH. Stop.

JENNY. We have each Landmark employee record a brief video in which they justify their jobs to us –

SETH. What? No no no. No. This is a slam-dunk growth play. An American family business, American designers, American-made. We'd be creating jobs right here in the US. Think about how helpful that would be right now.

(*To* JENNY.) What you're talking about – that is exactly why people hate us. Are you trying to make our situation worse?

JENNY. Do we work in public relations? Because I'm starting to feel like I accidentally work in public relations.

SETH (*ignoring her*). Let's agree to pull the trigger on this.

RICK. Yeah, you're talking me into it.

JENNY. He is?

SETH. With what's going on, this deal is perfect. It'll be great.

JENNY. It will *look* great.

RICK. Yeah.

JENNY. Can't argue with his plan looking great. But what I would point out, Rick, is the protests and the bad press will go away soon.

SETH. You don't know that.

RICK. I'm announcing a new foundation in Bali, gonna build a school there.

JENNY. See – exactly, a foundation in Bali.

SETH. Exactly what? / And if the protests don't stop

JENNY (*ignoring him*). / We need to focus on one thing: delivering the best possible return to our LPs. That's our job, nothing else.

SETH. What if these ShopGreat people don't give up? What if they get more people on their side? Say laws are changed. Say we suddenly have to pay income tax on carried interest. Have you actually thought about what that will mean for us?

JENNY. No, because that's ridiculous. Stop reading *BuzzFeed*.

RICK. Enough.

JENNY. I apologize.

SETH. Anyway.

RICK. We're talking about Landmark.

JENNY. Yes.

RICK. I have to decide.

JENNY. Here's why you say no to his plan.

RICK. I'm listening.

JENNY. Because this is what will happen: On Thursday, Seth's boyfriend Jeff Schrader will sign the LOI, and we'll sink six hundred grand into due diligence, that's a loss.

SETH. It's not a 'loss.'

JENNY. And then we execute the deal. Fine. Good. Great. Four-nine-one at twenty percent equity. We got a bargain. You're off *The Times* front page. You're back in the *Journal*. You're quoted about how private equity does in fact add value to American society cliché cliché cliché, generalization, cliché, and how we do in fact increase employment long term, cliché, main street, freedom, generalization, cliché, America.

RICK. I got it.

JENNY. But then. All we can do is sit there that first year and wait for the US consumer to suddenly fall in love with bespoke suitcases.

SETH. They aren't 'bespoke.'

JENNY. Your whole idea is made-to-order suitcases, is it not?

SETH. That's an oversimplification.

JENNY. Do you want me to look up bespoke for you in the dictionary?

SETH. No.

JENNY. Do you want me to look it up for you on my phone?

SETH. I know what it means.

JENNY. I have a dictionary on my phone, I'd be happy to look that up for you.

SETH. Why do you need a dictionary on your phone when you can just google a word on your phone?

RICK. Well that's enough of that.

JENNY (*to* RICK). Anyway, we wait. Revenue stays flat. I
    don't care about his analysts' projections saying that won't
    happen. Revenue will be flat.

SETH. You haven't even looked at our models.

JENNY. I don't have to. His analysts love him. They want to
    make him look good. My analysts? My analysts do not love
    me. That's how you know their numbers are real.

RICK. Get back to Landmark.

JENNY. And then we wait the next year, and revenue's still flat,
    because, after all, there's already a dominant player in the
    midmarket luggage sector. And then we wait another year,
    and we realize that we have, for some insane reason, put
    ourselves at the mercy of forces we can't control. We'll see
    that taking Landmark public was a fantasy. All of us will
    wonder how we exposed our LPs like this. And I bet our LPs
    will wonder about that as well. This could be a total wipeout.
    And how will we make up that loss elsewhere in the fund?

RICK. That sounds like a nightmare.

SETH. It won't happen with Landmark.

RICK. Still, it's high beta. Lot of contingencies.

SETH. I see how at first it seems riskier than we're used to, but
    actually, it's not. And Rick, online shopping has been a
    game-changing force, but no one has harnessed that force in
    the luggage industry. You know who shops online almost as
    much as women?

JENNY. You?

SETH. Men. And men go on business trips. And men like status
    objects, just as much as women do but they don't have
    nearly the indulgence vectors except in a few limited ways:
    watches, suits, phones –

JENNY. Cars.

SETH. Yes but cars are expensive. We're not going for that stratum. Those people have Louis Vuitton suitcases, Montblanc pens.

RICK. Those aren't comparable but go on.

SETH. This isn't for that demographic. This is for the guy who pulls down eighty-K in middle management, and it's Wednesday night and the Knicks game just ended and he's on the couch on his laptop and his wife's asleep, no sex again / and he's tooling around online feeling bored, feeling like a middle manager who pulls down eighty-K and he ends up on Landmark's site and there's all these cool ways to upgrade his travel gear. And he gets to customize it. He's in control. I can already see the one-sheet, checking in at his hotel with his Landmark rolling behind him and there's a beautiful woman standing by the check in counter and she's looking at him. Ten other people in the lobby and she's looking at him. //

JENNY. / Oh my gosh.

// Rick I'm worried about Seth.

SETH. Listen to her if you want. But we both know she's risk-averse.

JENNY. I'm risk-neutral.

SETH. You're risk-averse.

JENNY. You're math-averse.

SETH. She can't help it. Because they can bear children, women's brains have evolved to fear risk.

JENNY. Something you likely read in a magazine for the kind-of-smart-but-not-very-smart as you tried to relax on the cramped deck of your tiny boat.

SETH. How many times do I have to tell you, *Omar Coming* is a yacht.

RICK. When did you get a yacht?

SETH. Last year. We'd love to host you and Katie sometime.

RICK. That's okay.

SETH. Listen, six months ago when Jeff Schrader and I started talking seriously about this, I wasn't a hundred percent sure about it. But when my team ran the numbers, I said to myself: we have to do this.

RICK. What about seasonality?

SETH. Suitcases aren't a seasonal business. That's a myth.

JENNY. Yes. Rick, have you been to London in January? So fun to walk around in the ice rain.

SETH. Travel is seasonal. Suitcases aren't.

JENNY. And the two aren't linked?

SETH. No.

RICK. No?

SETH. Not when it comes to business travel.

JENNY. Most midmarket consumers buy one suitcase and use it for a decade.

SETH. What are you talking about?

Serious business travellers need new luggage every other year.

JENNY. That seems optimistic.

SETH. It's not. I went to Sacramento, I met with their head of sales. I can send you his data if you actually want know what you're talking about.

And let's remember, we're getting the business for four-nine-one at twenty percent.

RICK. We all agree it's a great price.

JENNY (*to* RICK). Okay, here's an idea: I'll run the numbers on a liquidation play.

SETH. That's not the concept, that's never been the concept. And gutting a functional American business is the very last thing we need to be doing right now.

RICK. Yes that's certainly true.

JENNY. So we do work in public relations.

RICK. Stop with that.

SETH. All she ever wants to do is strip companies down. She's biased.

JENNY. I am. I'm biased toward making decisions based on mathematical calculations, not on maudlin ideas about how the middle class feels on their sofas at night.

RICK. Stop, stop. Alright listen up –

RICK's *phone rings. He reads the caller ID.*

I gotta step out.

(*Answering.*) Morning! Or – good afternoon over there, I guess.

He leaves.

JENNY. What's going on?

SETH. I don't know.

JENNY. Who was that?

SETH. I don't know.

JENNY. It's clear he's not sleeping.

SETH. It's not escorts; he's done with that.

JENNY. Yeah.

SETH. He's really upset about the bad press.

JENNY. He's gotten bad press before.

SETH. Not on this scale.

JENNY. Fine, but since when is he so sensitive?

SETH. I think it's Katie.

JENNY. That wasn't Katie.

SETH. No, I'm saying maybe that's why this situation is even worse for him.

JENNY. Yeah.

SETH. But since when does he care that much about Katie?

JENNY. He did take that whole afternoon off when her contact lens rolled to the back of her eye.

SETH. Yeah.

JENNY. And he's marrying her.

SETH. He married Jeanine.

JENNY. That was different. I don't think he even liked Jeanine.

SETH. Yeah. Jeanine was a manipulative genius.

JENNY. Wait you don't think Katie's a genius?

They share a look.

SETH. She's a sweet girl though.

JENNY. He's getting soft.

SETH. No, he's having a commensurate response to a major crisis.

JENNY. It's not a major crisis.

SETH. It actually is. We live in a democracy.

JENNY. Thanks I didn't know that.

SETH. If you make too many people too mad, they can change things.

JENNY. Can they though?

SETH. Yes. They can. Ask France.

JENNY. What?

SETH. You tip the scales too far? You rub your wealth in their faces? The people will rise up. Ask France.

JENNY. Ask France?

SETH. Yeah.

JENNY. What does that even mean?

SETH. You go too far, you have the French Revolution on your hands.

JENNY. What? Sorry, what do you think caused the French Revolution?

SETH. Income inequality was too severe.

JENNY. Oh no.

SETH. Not exclusively that. I'm making a point.

JENNY. How do I always forget you went to Montessori school?

SETH. Why are you trying to stop this deal? It's ninety-eight-point-two from the fund. That's nothing.

JENNY. I'm gonna google the French Revolution for you.

SETH. Every minute that goes by, we risk another firm jumping on this.

JENNY. Do other firms know they'll do four-nine-one?

SETH. No, that price is just for us.

JENNY. Then we don't risk them jumping on this.

SETH. Don't think I don't know what you're doing.

JENNY. What I'm doing is trying to keep us from being tied down to literally the *Titanic* of investments.

SETH. Literally the *Titanic*? Really? So we're standing at the bottom of the North Atlantic right now and I'm trying to tie you to a boat.

JENNY. I love it when you critique things that don't matter.

SETH. That's literally the meaning of what you just said.

JENNY. It's a perfect example of your null value to the firm.

SETH. I don't see how even you don't see the potential here. And at this price, we aren't exposing the fund to / nearly the risk you're

JENNY. / Alright alright, stop. Just stop talking. It doesn't matter. A company with these assets four-nine-one? He's gonna buy it. It doesn't matter what I say.

SETH. That's right. That's right.

JENNY. How did you get that price?

SETH. I had Jeff Schrader talk to Stu. Jeff likes me. I know no one has ever liked you before, probably not even when you were an infant.

JENNY. I was a very advanced infant.

SETH. I'm sure. If you know this deal is happening then why are you fighting it?

JENNY. Let's talk about how your growth play will hurt our image.

SETH. What?

JENNY. Everyone in our world will wonder why Rick allowed us to get entangled in a plan this complicated.

SETH. Jenny, it's not that complicated. Maybe it seems that way to you because you're not as intelligent as me.

JENNY. I got a seven-sixty on the GMAT. You?

SETH. Seven-seventy.

JENNY. No you didn't.

SETH. Yes I did.

JENNY. No you didn't.

SETH. Yes I did.

JENNY. You got a seven-fifty.

SETH. No. Seven-seventy.

JENNY. I remember that day. You got a seven-fifty.

SETH. That's weird. You're wrong. As usual.

JENNY. I'm having an assistant call Wharton this afternoon.

SETH. To ask them my GMAT score?

JENNY. Yes.

SETH. That's insane.

JENNY. Here is one of the many things that bother me about this idea: I know your greatest passion in life is trying to force this firm to behave as a charitable organization, not a / business, but

SETH. / That's not at all true. This growth play will make us a lot of money.

JENNY. It will almost certainly not make us as much money as possible. And if it appears that he's trying to grow Landmark so the press will stop being mean to us, that's not good, Seth. Who in their right mind will invest with us if they think Rick is choosing deals because they're emotionally appealing to people in the media who don't understand anything about what we do in the first place?

SETH. You didn't get a seven-sixty.

JENNY. I actually did. You don't get into HBS with anything below ninety-ninth percentile.

SETH. You do if you're a....

JENNY. If you're a....?

SETH. If you have a gender strength.

JENNY (*getting out her phone*). I'm logging into my GMAT account right now.

SETH. Okay, I don't care.

JENNY. Seth backs down. What a surprise twist. I'm still logging in.

(*As she does this*.) By the way, shrewd of you to hide the price from me till now.

SETH. Thank you.

JENNY. This could really be a beautiful transaction.

See. Seven-sixty.

SETH. My score minus ten, congratulations.

Landmark is an opportunity for value creation, not whatever financial engineering bullshit you're probably thinking about right now.

JENNY. You have no idea what I'm thinking about right now.

SETH. We need to buy companies, increase their value, then exit, that's it.

JENNY (*tuning him out*). I am annoyed that he won't at least let me run the numbers on a liquidation play.

SETH. That is an absurd idea. We're only even discussing this deal because of my and Jeff's plan.

JENNY. You and Jeff. Question: Does Rebecca know about you two?

SETH. That's so funny. I'm not offended by that joke, but GUESS WHAT homophobia and misogyny are the fruit of the same tree. So you're a bird flying into her own cage and laughing at the bars.

JENNY. On my list of top American poets, it goes Toni Morrison number one, you number two.

SETH. Toni Morrison is a novelist.

JENNY. You are. So soft.

SETH. Keep it up. You will lose. Because I actually bring in deals and I give him creative ideas. I'm a leader. I have vision. You have nothing. You're a vampire.

JENNY. Seth, I'm afraid you don't understand the nuances of finance.

SETH. I'm afraid you don't understand the nuances of finance.

JENNY. You have terrible instincts and middling ambition.

SETH. You are a token hire with sociopathic tendencies.

JENNY. There is a hawk on my shoulder. You can't see it, but it is always there.

And for that reason, I never relax and I never take a moment to just enjoy the moment. This gives me a permanent advantage.

One day you will be at a dinner party, and you'll be trying to think of something insightful to say because it means so much to you to be liked, but the conversation will be about something unfamiliar, so you'll just be sitting there with that look you always have.

And at that moment, or a comparable moment, I will destroy you.

SETH. There's a what on your shoulder?

RICK *returns*.

RICK. Alright. Anyway –

JENNY. Is everything okay?

SETH. Was that one our LPs?

JENNY. Was it the Beckwiths?

RICK (*ignoring their questions*). Seth, a growth play like this is always risky.

SETH. Not this time. Not when you dig into the projections.

RICK. But that price.

SETH. Yeah.

RICK. We have to buy it.

SETH. Yes. That's the right call.

RICK. Can't say no to four-nine-one.

JENNY. Yeah.

RICK. But, maybe we want a management plan that's not so...

JENNY. Out there.

RICK. The right play here might be more conservative.

JENNY. I agree.

SETH. Can I just say one thing?

RICK. Absolutely not.

(*To* JENNY.) Bring me another option. Nothing extreme. I'm wondering: What happens if we keep the company as is, but we execute some easy cuts?

(*To* SETH.) Their suitcases are made in America?

SETH. In California. That's important to Jeff.

RICK. Let's look at what happens if we offshore production. Or nearshore – Mexico.

SETH. Rick, I've looked into Mexican luggage suppliers.

RICK. Quiet.

(*To* JENNY.) Do run the numbers on that.

JENNY. Okay.

RICK. But keep management in California, and non-production payroll stays intact.

JENNY. Rick –

RICK. Show me cuts that allow continuity – nothing that will disrupt management or harm the brand.

JENNY. Alright. But I do want to emphasize that this seems like an opportunity to / aggressively cut

RICK. / I said no. I'm not gutting this suitcase company at a
time when the Gjertsons' investment manager can't enter his
office in Oslo without encountering the spraypainted image
of a US dollar sign dripping blood onto a stick figure meant
to represent the working class.

SETH. Sorry, what?

RICK. This morning. Spraypainted right by the front door.

JENNY. What was the image again? I didn't track all of that.

RICK. It was in solidarity with the ShopGreat employees.

JENNY. Ex-employees. Who in Norway cares about some laid-
off American supermarket cashiers?

RICK. Apparently they read *The Times* in Oslo.

SETH. Are the Gjertsons upset?

RICK. I sent a gift. It was cleaned up quickly.

JENNY. Good.

SETH. But we can't let this continue.

RICK. No.

SETH. And that's why my and Jeff's growth play is the magic
bullet for us right now.

JENNY. It's paint. It's paint on a wall.

RICK (*to* JENNY). Enough.

JENNY. I apologize.

RICK. Go get your team on this.

    I want projections for offshoring and continuity, nothing
    else.

JENNY. Alright.

    She goes.

SETH. If I can just clarify one thing, moving manufacturing
offshore, even just to Mexico, it / isn't actually

RICK (*looking at his phone*). / Hold on I need to read this.

He reads it. SETH *waits.* RICK *finishes reading it.*

RICK *throws the phone against the wall. Then he smashes it to pieces.*

SETH. Everything okay?

RICK. Is Michael out there?

SETH *goes.*

He returns.

SETH. Yeah.

RICK. Ask him to order me a new one please.

SETH *goes.*

He returns.

SETH. It'll be here in forty minutes.

RICK. Thank you.

SETH. Everything okay?

RICK. Yep.

Beat.

Why are you still here Seth?

SETH. We can't put Landmark through those cuts.

RICK. If we buy it, we can do whatever we want with it.

SETH. Of course. But offshoring production would mean significant job loss in Sacramento, which is not something we can have our hand in right now.

RICK. I built my reputation on strong returns. I achieve strong returns because I consider deals from opposing angles. That is why I employ both you and her.

SETH. Of course, but this / is different

RICK. / That's my thing. Thought you'd know that by now. Ask Michael to send you that Forbes profile on my management philosophy. He has a PDF.

SETH. I know. It's just: our current situation? This is her fault. She failed you. She advised you to go ahead with a million-dollar engagement party with elephants / on the same day we laid off thousands of ShopGreat employees. Thousands of people. Jobs they'd had for decades. The way out of this isn't her way, it's my way. //

RICK. / One elephant.

// I'm not considering her way.

SETH. Okay, I'm sorry. It's just been a few months now, talking through this with Jeff Schrader and Stu. They trust me.

RICK. I know. That's valuable. So how much debt is this gonna be for them?

SETH. Three-hundred-and-ninety-two-point-eight million.

RICK. That's a lot for a company this size.

SETH. All of our cases keep Landmark clear of bankruptcy.

RICK. We don't know for a fact that there's consumer demand for customizable suitcases.

SETH. I mean that's technically true, yeah. But of course, Adolphus Green didn't know that there was consumer demand for the Oreo. But that dude went ahead and made a fucking Oreo.

RICK *looks at him*.

I'm sorry. That got away from me a little bit.

RICK. You want to come up with cookie concepts?

SETH. What?

RICK. Is that what you want to do for a living?

SETH. No.

RICK. What do you want to do for a living?

SETH. I wanna be here. I wanna do deals.

RICK. Do you?

SETH. Yes.

RICK. Don't fall in love with details.

SETH. What are we gonna say to Jeff Schrader on Thursday?

RICK. Nothing. He signs the letter, and that's it.

SETH. He doesn't know offshoring is on the table.

RICK. Good.

SETH. Stu and Jeff didn't intend for 491 to be the price
    regardless of our management plan.

RICK. Then they should have gotten that in writing.

SETH. Okay. Yeah. This makes me a little uncomfortable.

RICK. Sorry to hear that. Now I need a moment.

SETH. Okay. Sorry, but even if it's unlikely, I don't know if I
    can stop myself from telling Jeff that offshoring is on the
    table.

RICK. You said, what now? You said you don't know if you can
    stop yourself?

SETH. I think we could do real harm to ourselves if we aren't
    careful right now.

RICK. You said: You don't know if you can stop yourself from
    fucking up my deal. I can help you with that, Seth. I know
    that you will stop yourself. Who am I?

SETH. Yeah, you're my boss.

RICK. No who am I?

SETH. You're Rick Hannel.

RICK. Who am I to you?

SETH. My friend?

RICK. Way off. Who am I?

SETH. I don't know.

RICK. You don't know? Okay. I'm the guy who made you. I'm the guy who chose you out of all the summer analysts, who told you what kind of tie to buy, who valued your deal-sourcing skills, who chose you and only you – aside from her – to come here and start this firm with me. That's the story of how I made you.

SETH. Okay. / Yes.

RICK. / It took years. But I can unmake you in five seconds.

SETH. I know.

RICK. You found a good deal. You were right about the party. That doesn't mean you get to act like I took your Barbie away because I want to compare your growth play to other operating models.

SETH. I'm sorry.

RICK. When have I ever done a deal without considering a variety of management plans?

SETH. I just thought you wouldn't consider offshoring at a time like this.

RICK. At a time like this. So you think I'm scared. You think I'm the sort of guy who abandons his principles when I'm under pressure. Is that what you think of me?

SETH. Of course not. I won't say anything to Jeff. I won't say anything.

Lights.

3.

Wednesday evening.

A hotel bar.

JEFF SCHRADER *stands holding a beer in a nice glass.*

JEFF *reads a luggage-industry quarterly.*

SETH *arrives.*

JEFF. Hey man.

SETH. There he is.

> JEFF *initiates a hug.*

> Good flight?

JEFF. Oh man.

SETH. Right?

JEFF. I was dead against buying that jet, plus I'm really into my Delta status, you know, / but

SETH. / Your what?

JEFF. My Delta status. I'm at Diamond.

SETH. Oh. Is that a high level?

JEFF. It's the highest.

SETH. Whoa, I did not know who I was talking to.

JEFF. Yeah dude. Diamond.

> But seriously, coming out here today, I mean there's no security line –

SETH. You save a ton of time. And no one tells you what to do.

JEFF. Oh yeah I was on the phone with Dana during takeoff.

SETH. This guy just does not care.

JEFF. It's crazy. I didn't know what I was missing. Anyway. Hey. It's all happening. I was saying to Dana, I can't believe this week is finally here.

SETH. I know. Yeah. Crazy.

JEFF. Everything good with you?

SETH. Yeah. Yeah honestly, I'm fucking tired. Rebecca wasn't feeling well last night.

JEFF. How's she doing?

SETH. She's good, she's doing fine, just gets nauseous sometimes.

JEFF. Oh yeah, Dana had that. But you guys must be so stoked.

SETH. Yeah.

JEFF. You got a name yet?

SETH. My mom's father was named Barrington, he was an important guy to me. So we were thinking Barrington might be cool.

JEFF. It's a baby girl right?

SETH. Yeah we could call her Bear, I don't know.

JEFF. Bear might be a tricky name for a girl.

SETH. Maybe, I don't know.

JEFF. No that's cool, that's so exciting man.

SETH. Yeah.

JEFF. How are things at the firm?

SETH. Good, good.

JEFF. I saw that thing in *The Times*.

SETH. Oh. Yeah. That's been a whole thing this week.

JEFF. Yeah.

SETH. I told him that morning when it was clear what the optics would be – I looked in his eyes and I said you have to cancel the fucking party.

JEFF. Yeah.

SETH. He didn't listen to me.

JEFF. Right.

SETH. I do feel bad about the folks who lost their jobs.

JEFF. Yeah. That's a lot of people. That's brutal.

SETH. But, you know. I'm sure you get it. Those layoffs were a function of years of bad management. It was bound to happen no matter who bought them out.

JEFF. Sure.

SETH. This media stuff gets to the point where it's so one-sided.

JEFF. He threw a party. Who doesn't like parties?

SETH. Exactly. I mean he shouldn't have.

JEFF. Of course.

SETH. But did he kill someone?

JEFF. No.

SETH. But listen, this shit poses no threat to the deal. We are buying Landmark.

JEFF. Tell you what, I'm ready to finally put this in motion. I've been on Stu to modernize Landmark for years.

SETH. I know.

JEFF. And on my end personally, you know, it's just in time.

SETH. Oh yeah. We'll fix that right up. I don't know why you accepted something so low.

JEFF. Stu was taking a chance when he hired me.

SETH. Yeah but a two percent raise scheme over the past decade –

JEFF. Yeah, I know.

SETH. And those tiny bonuses? That's totally outside the norm for someone in your role.

JEFF. At one point, something bigger was in the works, a few years ago, that's partly why Dana and I bought the winery.

SETH. Dancing Sun.

JEFF. Moon. Dancing Moon.

But then the downturn hit.

SETH. California real estate is bouncing back though, right?

JEFF. Yeah, slowly in that part but yeah.

SETH. How's the winery going?

JEFF. It's not great – we're on pause right now until we can pay workers, but we're planning. We're planning.

SETH. That's cool man.

JEFF. Yeah it's cool. It's a money pit, but it's cool.

SETH. We'll renegotiate your salary right after close.

JEFF. Oh – Ted got back to me.

SETH. Ted?

JEFF. The suitcase designer here.

SETH. Oh yeah.

JEFF. He has some customizable samples we can look at.

SETH. Oh, okay cool. I'll find some time for that.

JEFF. You can bring your colleagues, maybe Rick?

SETH. He'll probably be too busy.

JEFF. The pictures looked really promising. I mean Ted's giving us quarter-inch customizability on height, depth and width.

Think about all the business travelers who have to pack
weird shit – presentation materials, product samples, medical
device sales –

SETH. Yeah

JEFF. I hear from them all the time. No one's serving those
people.

SETH. Till now. Maybe I can get Rick to come. He doesn't
usually deal with details at this stage.

JEFF. Sure, this is in your silo.

SETH. He'll be more involved after close.

JEFF. Okay, yeah. I'm sure he has his way of doing things.

SETH. Yeah. By the way, Jeff, if Rick has any ideas about our
plan, what would you think about that?

JEFF. I guess I'd have to know what kind of ideas.

SETH. Say maybe we do go ahead with the plan to make
Landmark online-only, but we don't have customizable
products, I don't know.

JEFF. So our inventory would be what? Our current line?

SETH. No, no it's a hypothetical. I'm saying, if Rick were to
change our plan in that way, for example, what would you
think about that?

JEFF. I mean, I'm a grown man, I know this is a buyout. But I
feel like, after these months talking with you, there's a trust
here.

SETH. I agree. And if this thing takes off like I think it will,
there's a decent shot you'll be on the cover of *Businessweek*
in the next couple years.

JEFF. Ah no.

SETH. I'm serious.

JEFF. But listen, my take is, if you're gonna be working with
me, then this is gonna be a net positive for everyone.

SETH. Yeah I feel the same way.

JEFF. It was funny, with the media all over Rick this week, I had to reassure a few friends back in Cali – they'd read some articles about ShopGreat and people harassing your investors and all that shit.

SETH. Right.

JEFF. I told them, look this is a top-tier firm.

SETH. I mean, we're not Diamond status like you.

JEFF. Few are dude. Few are. But you know, I was saying to people back home: it looks like ShopGreat had major problems. Crazy over-expansion.

SETH. Yeah.

JEFF. We're not in that situation, fortunately, but Landmark does need change.

SETH. Sure.

JEFF. It wasn't till you guys came along that I even thought this was possible.

SETH. It's a great investment for us.

JEFF. And seriously: I know you'll come to me if there's anything I need to know.

SETH. I will Jeff, absolutely. You have my word on that.

JEFF. Hey. It's all happening.

SETH. Yeah. You feel good?

JEFF. Yeah man.

SETH. You ready to sign this thing tomorrow?

JEFF. Yeah dude. It's about time. Hey, let me buy you a drink.

SETH. I'd love to but I have shit to do.

JEFF *gets up to go to the bar.*

JEFF. Just one.

SETH. Okay.

Lights.

4.

Thursday.

KMM Capital Management.

JENNY, SETH, RICK.

JENNY has two folders.

On a table, the Letter of Intent.

SETH. We can't keep him waiting.

JENNY. This won't take long. Where is he?

SETH. We left him by reception.

JENNY. Where were you guys?

RICK. Downtown.

JENNY. Doing what?

SETH. Jeff Schrader had a luggage designer do some customizable mock-ups.

JENNY *(to* RICK*)*. You went downtown to look at suitcases?

RICK. Yes.

SETH *(to* RICK*)*. Interesting stuff. Thanks again for breakfast, that was really nice.

 RICK *reads an email.*

RICK. Jenny, go ahead.

JENNY. I'll wait for you to…

RICK. When I say go ahead, go ahead.

JENNY. I apologize. I've been working twenty-seven hours straight.

SETH. Is John okay?

RICK. Who?

JENNY. Nine Johns work here Seth.

SETH. John Kim. Your analyst.

JENNY. Oh, yeah.

SETH. Is he out of the hospital?

RICK. What happened?

SETH. Too much Adderall.

I heard you wouldn't let him leave.

JENNY. He'll be fine.

SETH. Is that why Sam was crying?

RICK. She's still in the building?

SETH. Yeah we walked by her on the way in.

JENNY. Who's crying?

SETH. Sam.

JENNY. Sam from PR?

SETH. Yeah.

RICK. I fired Sam.

SETH. What?

RICK (*to* JENNY). Is your analyst out of the hospital?

JENNY. I don't know.

RICK. Well the firm should send him something. Where does
   he live?

JENNY. I don't know.

SETH. He's worked for you for three years.

JENNY. And?

RICK. Okay, Jenny go ahead.

JENNY. Alright. Let me gather my thoughts.

RICK. Here sit down.

JENNY. I am sitting down.

She's not.

SETH. No you're standing.

JENNY. I think I know when I'm standing.

Rick, my analysts and I went through the Landmark material. And it's clear why they want to sell quickly: flat net sales, runaway costs in almost every department.

SETH. Yes, it needs a new business model. That's literally my exact plan.

JENNY. Seth your plan would return two-point-eight to three-point-two times our invested capital.

SETH. That's right.

JENNY. And that's fine I guess.

SETH. It's excellent.

JENNY. It's fine. But I can hit three-point-five.

RICK. How?

JENNY. We purchase Landmark for four-nine-one. Same capital structure. Upon close, we immediately list their jet. Landmark will spend not one dollar more maintaining that albatross. Pun intended.

SETH. That's not a pun.

JENNY (*ignoring him*). Then, we stop production, and move manufacturing to Bangladesh.

SETH. What?

RICK. I said Mexico.

JENNY. Bangladesh is far less expensive.

RICK. But when you factor in shipping costs.

JENNY. Yes, but here's the twist: suitcases produced in Bangladesh will not be shipped to the United States.

SETH. What?

JENNY. We'll sell to the emerging middle-class consumers in China.

RICK. China?

JENNY. China.

SETH. China's economy is completely stalled.

JENNY. China still offers the hope of a growing middle class. That's not something American consumers can give us anymore.

SETH. Sorry your plan is based on hope?

JENNY. In 2020, thirty percent of all urban households in China will be upper-middle-class, compared to seventeen percent today. American investors will kill to find a way into that market.

SETH. That's a huge assumption to make.

JENNY. We're in the business of exiting investments. We exit an investment when we find a buyer for a business we own. I have in my office a five-page single-spaced list of private equity firms sitting on way too much capital right now. Firms that are starving for deals. Our peers will fall all over themselves to buy this China-oriented Landmark from us. Why? Because they have to buy something. Even if only to have an asset they can flip themselves in a few years. We know that as well as anyone.

RICK. What if Landmark struggles in a new market? Could risk bankruptcy.

JENNY. Not within the next eight years. We'll be long gone by then. And so will the next owner, if they're smart.

SETH. You are drowning.

JENNY. I'm not. During the shift to China, we'll have Landmark establish a holding company, which Jeff Schrader will use to issue a hundred million in new debt.

SETH. No.

JENNY. Yes.

SETH. From where?

JENNY. Probably a hedge fund, maybe your friend at Prism Capital.

SETH. He won't do that unless I ask.

JENNY. Then we'll ask someone else. It's Rick, it's only a hundred million. And from that hundred million, Landmark will pay us a special dividend of ninety-eight-point-two million dollars.

RICK. Our equity off the table.

JENNY. That's right. Our money back in a matter of months. At this point, we'd have nothing at risk.

SETH. What if Jeff refuses to do any of that?

JENNY. I did mention the bonus.

RICK. You didn't.

JENNY. I apologize, I'm tired. As soon as the deal closes, we'll offer him a bonus so he'll stick around.

SETH. So he'll stick around?

JENNY. Factoring in our skinny equity check, our dividend, the cost efficiencies we'll capture when we move production, and the bidding war we'll cause when we're ready to exit, my analysts and I have determined that we'll hit three-point-five times our invested capital, with no risk of a wipeout.

RICK. Three-point-five.

JENNY. And it could possibly hit three-point-seven. I didn't have time to get my team to run a full cost analysis on shipping routes. One of my guys went down last night.

RICK. John, right?

JENNY. John Wright? I guess that's his name. He's Korean-American.

SETH. Yikes. It's 10:03. Are we done humoring her now?

RICK. Hold on. How would Landmark service all that debt in the short term?

JENNY. My analysts ran sensitivities.

RICK. Including the dividend recap? You'd be forcing a highly leveraged company to take on more debt.

SETH. Just to pay ourselves.

JENNY. Landmark will be able to make its payments in the short term.

RICK. How?

JENNY. The details are in here.

RICK. Give me broad strokes.

JENNY. Okay. Landmark will sell its US warehouses to Amazon, that's around twenty-five million.

And Dole Foods is looking to move its corporate offices to Sacramento to be closer to its state lobbyists. They'll pay a premium to lease the Landmark building.

RICK. Interesting.

SETH. And then where would we put Landmark's employees?

JENNY. In a suburban office space. I've already priced the rent on that.

SETH. All six hundred and fifty-three non-production employees would move to a suburban office space?

JENNY. Not all of them.

RICK. What do you mean, not all of them?

JENNY. In my plan, a lot of Landmark jobs in California become unnecessary.

SETH. Here we go.

RICK. How many?

JENNY. The numbers are in there.

RICK. How many?

JENNY. In Sacramento, Landmark will retain three executives,
one accountant and a receptionist. Plus we'll want to hire a
VP for Asia.

SETH. So Landmark will have six employees.

JENNY. In California. Obviously we'd employ workers in
Bangladesh and we'd set up a small staff in China.

SETH. This is fucking absurd.

JENNY. What's absurd is overspending to execute your plan,
when mine is better.

RICK. Jenny.

JENNY. Yes.

RICK. This is not what I asked you for.

JENNY (*to* RICK). You asked for a plan that maintains the
current operating model, but outsources production to a
Mexican supplier. There it is. As you'll see, the best we
could do is one-point-seven. That's even worse than his
projected return.

SETH. Are we done listening to this? I need to bring Jeff in.

JENNY. I think I've made my case, Rick. Now, I'm gonna go
lay down.

She's starting to lie down.

RICK (*a preventive sound*). Sit here.

JENNY. Okay, yes.

SETH (*to* JENNY). You're really having an off week. Maybe
take a vacation?

JENNY. Vacations are for expendable people. Like you.

RICK (*to* SETH). Go get Jeff Schrader.

SETH *goes*.

JENNY *offers* RICK *a folder*.

JENNY. Here are all the cases for my plan.

RICK. I don't want it.

JENNY. This is a guaranteed three-point-five versus a
    contingent two-point-eight to three-point-two on his side.

RICK. I don't care.

JENNY. I apologize, but I'm shocked that you'd reject this.

RICK. I do not care about a few extra points.

JENNY. Okay. Rick, I'm starting to worry.

RICK. Sorry to hear that.

JENNY. We could destroy our reputation if we do his dumb
    website idea when we could clearly have made more money
    my way.

RICK. We can make what your way?

JENNY. More money. It's three-point-five versus two-point-
    eight to three-point-two. That's a difference of at least
    twenty million dollars.

RICK. Twenty million.

JENNY. At least.

RICK. Here's a numbers question for you. Are you ready?

JENNY. Always.

RICK. Is a few million extra on Landmark worth losing
    hundreds of millions over the next decade because no family
    office, no university endowment, no pension fund will invest
    with us, ever again?

JENNY. That won't happen.

RICK. It's already happening.

JENNY. What?

RICK. Your plan isn't lucrative. It's expensive.

JENNY. What do you mean it's already happening?

SETH *returns with* JEFF.

JEFF. Hey there.

RICK. Hello again.

JEFF. Thanks for coming to check out Ted's pieces this morning.

RICK. Really interesting stuff, I enjoyed it.

This is Jenny. Jenny's our other founding director.

JEFF. Of course, yeah. Nice to finally meet. How's it going?

JENNY. We've heard so much about you.

JEFF. Good things I hope.

JENNY. Yes.

SETH. This guy's a superstar.

JEFF. And people always say you New York people aren't nice.

RICK. I've never understood that stereotype myself.

JEFF. At our Volunteer Saturday last weekend, I was serving soup with my head of HR Barbara, and she was all 'carry your money in your front pocket' and I was like Barb it's not like that anymore. Hasn't been like that for years.

RICK. Oh yeah, it's a different city now.

JEFF. She's from an older generation.

JENNY. Volunteer Saturday?

SETH. Yeah. Landmark employees volunteer together twice a year. Jeff's initiative.

JENNY. You pay them to volunteer?

JEFF. Oh no they aren't paid, it's optional.

JENNY. And they still come?

SETH. It's usually a big turnout right?

JEFF. Yeah yeah, most of my people show up.

JENNY. Why do they come?

JEFF. I guess they like helping out, you know.

JENNY. I don't understand.

SETH. They come because Jeff asks them to. They respect him.

JEFF. But also it's kinda fun. Everyone gets to see each other in shorts.

RICK. Start up a couple office romances.

JEFF. I think there may have been a couple of those over the years.

RICK. Occupational hazard. Alright, let's get you sorted out here, please sit.

Jeff, there are two more steps before the deal can be executed. Right now, we sign the Letter of Intent.

(*To* SETH.) I understand Jeff is the authorized signee.

SETH. That's correct.

RICK. Aside from the LOI, all that's left is the remainder of the due-diligence process. Bain people will be reaching out to Landmark's executive team. Just simple interviews, about the company, about what they do in their jobs.

JENNY. And obviously they'll want to see any numbers you haven't given us.

RICK. After due diligence, as long as the financing is settled on our end, we'll close on Landmark. Does that square with your understanding?

JEFF. Yes, yeah it does.

RICK. You'll want to give your managers a heads-up about the due diligence.

JEFF. Oh, they know. I actually called a company-wide meeting, to let everyone know this deal was going to happen. I didn't want my people hearing about it the wrong way.

JENNY. What did you tell them?

JEFF. I didn't get into details, but I did communicate that this would mean growth for the company, as opposed to cuts. I don't want people worrying for no reason.

SETH. That's right.

RICK. That's important.

JEFF. When Seth and I mapped out how we'll keep everyone on board, it was a huge weight off my shoulders.

JENNY. We can discuss details at a later date.

RICK. Okay. We ready to do this?

SETH. Yeah.

JEFF. I had one thought this morning, if it's okay to ask.

SETH. Of course.

RICK. Please. Now's the time.

JEFF. I know both sets of lawyers have gone back and forth on this thing a thousand times. I don't wanna bum people out.

SETH. Jeff you're incapable of bumming people out.

RICK. This is why I wanted us all to get in a room together, to get on the same page.

JEFF. I had a thought about the Letter of Intent. Would it be possible to amend it one more time?

RICK. Sure. What are you thinking?

JEFF. It would be great if I could come back to my people in Sacramento and be able to say, look, right here in the Letter of Intent, there's a guarantee that none of the changes at Landmark are gonna cost you your jobs.

JENNY. You want a clause about that in the LOI?

JEFF. Something like that, if it's possible.

JENNY. It's not.

SETH. He's just asking.

JENNY. We can't commit to a management plan in an LOI.

JEFF. Okay, I hear you. What about a separate agreement about that?

JENNY. Regardless of what the document is titled, you must understand that we can't tie ourselves to an operating model at this stage. What if there's another recession in two years? What if, out of nowhere, the FAA outlaws suitcases on commercial aircraft?

SETH. What are you talking about?

JEFF. As I said, I hear you. I'm certainly not asking for a detailed plan.

RICK. And that's understood, Jeff. It's a fair question on your part.

How about this? Our lawyers are down on Sixteen. They can get your legal team on video conference, and maybe you all can come up with an addendum that will satisfy what you're looking for. That sound acceptable?

JEFF. Yeah, absolutely. I really appreciate it.

SETH. I'll take you down there, get that set up.

JEFF. Thanks so much for hearing me out on this.

RICK. Thanks for looking out for your employees. I respect that, Jeff, I do.

JEFF. Once this is settled, I'm ready to pull the trigger.

RICK. Great.

JEFF (*to* JENNY *and* RICK). Oh – hey can I get your addresses?

JENNY. Why?

JEFF. You're about to join the Landmark family – I'd love to send you some of my favorite pieces.

SETH. Rebecca and I have a couple, they're great.

RICK. How nice, thank you Jeff. You can ship them to the office.

JEFF (*to* JENNY). Do you prefer soft-side or hard-side?

JENNY. What?

JEFF. For your suitcase.

JENNY. I don't need a new suitcase.

RICK (*to* SETH). Alright.

SETH. Let's get that set up.

RICK. Seth, come right back up please.

SETH. Okay.

    SETH *and* JEFF *go*. RICK *reads something on his phone*.

JENNY. Amateur hour.

RICK. He, like most CEOs, is nervous at this stage, and all you did was make it worse.

JENNY. I apologize.

RICK. And you can't accept a free suitcase?

JENNY. I own a complete luggage set.

RICK. That is not the point.

JENNY. I know. I apologize. Maybe I should take a vacation. I've always kind of wanted to fly over Antarctica and look out the window. I'd be back in a day.

RICK. No, we have some things to deal with.

SETH *returns*.

SETH. Legal's gonna take him back to his hotel after he's done.

JENNY. Hopefully he won't get sidetracked by a volunteering opportunity on the way there.

SETH. Sorry, you're making fun of him because he volunteers?

RICK. I think it's an indication of a strong leader. That he gets his people to do that with him.

SETH. Me too.

RICK. Is this going to be a problem?

SETH. No, we'll get him to sign it.

RICK. You sure?

SETH. Yes.

RICK. Why did he ask for that?

SETH. He's in that nervous phase. It'll be fine. I'll talk to him. We'll get it signed.

RICK. Good.

SETH. I'll have him come back in tomorrow morning.

RICK. Tomorrow morning won't work.

SETH. Why not?

JENNY. We need him to sign.

RICK. Once he signs, due diligence will move quickly on this.

SETH. Yeah, it's already started.

RICK (*to* SETH). Can you call Bain? Tell them they can take it slow.

SETH. Oh. Okay.

JENNY. Why?

RICK. I don't have the money to buy Landmark right now.

SETH. What?

JENNY. No, you do. It's ninety-eight-point-two and we have three-seventy in dry powder.

RICK. We don't have three-seventy.

JENNY. We do.

RICK. We don't. Have your assistants pack you for Hong Kong.

SETH. What?

RICK. Wheels up from Teterboro at 6 a.m. tomorrow.

SETH. Sorry, Hong Kong?

JENNY. What's going on?

SETH. What's in Hong Kong?

JENNY. Xu Wei?

RICK. I called Xu Wei this morning.

SETH. Why?

JENNY. Are you gonna take a commitment from Xu Wei?

RICK. We're launching a new fund.

SETH. But he's a slimeball.

RICK. This is what we're doing.

SETH. Why?

RICK. I just told you. We don't have the money to do this deal.

JENNY. What happened to our fund?

RICK. Jenny, you said none of our LPs will stop investing with us?

JENNY. Look at our recent returns.

SETH. What happened?

RICK. They're refusing the capital call.

JENNY. What? They can't do that.

RICK. They can.

JENNY. They can't.

SETH. They signed the agreement.

RICK. The agreement allows our LPs to terminate the fund if they vote to do so.

JENNY. Only if a four-fifths super-majority votes to terminate.

RICK. Well, every LP wants to terminate. So I guess they have their super-majority.

SETH. Jesus Christ.

RICK. They're putting out press releases tomorrow, together, to draw attention to the fact that they're walking away from us.

JENNY. But they'll have to pay a huge penalty.

RICK. They're paying it.

JENNY. They're wasting their own capital. That's idiotic.

RICK. That's public relations.

SETH. Holy shit.

RICK. I did everything I could to talk them out of it.

JENNY. How did this happen?

RICK. It started with the Beckwith Trust.

JENNY. I knew they couldn't handle it.

RICK. And then the Snyder office joined them.

SETH. What about the Gjertsons?

JENNY. Yeah the Gjertsons are happy, Jan wants in on our next fund.

RICK. Not anymore.

SETH. They're gonna connect us with the oil-fund guys.

RICK. Not anymore. I spent how many years building a relationship with the Gjertsons' investment team, and now they won't take my calls. They didn't even acknowledge the fruit and wine basket I sent three days ago.

SETH. Wow.

JENNY. I am going to go to my office because I do not want anyone to observe me crying.

RICK. Stay here.

JENNY. I've never heard of protests being this effective.

RICK. This is what they wanted. People know the Landmark deal is in the works. They want humiliation. Anyway, we're down to nineteen million, and that's our own money. We need at least eighty from Xu Wei, just to close on Landmark.

JENNY. But you said you'd never let him into a fund.

SETH. He's been denaturalized by the Chinese government.

RICK. This is what we're doing.

SETH. Rick. Xu Wei has done some really questionable things.

RICK. Between not being able to do this deal and taking him on as an LP, I've chosen the lesser of two evils.

SETH. Okay. Understood. And I'm not trying to act like you took my Barbie away, and I respect your procedure, but let's confirm: if we're really going to take his money, we have to go with my plan.

RICK. As long as he allocates at least eighty, we'll close on Landmark.

SETH. I know but after close, we have to go with the growth play. No offshoring, no cuts.

JENNY. Actually –

SETH. It's even more important now than it was before.

JENNY. Actually –

RICK. I'm considering the deal from every angle.

JENNY. If Xu Wei commits eighty or more, then he'll become our most important LP. And if he becomes our most important LP, then we're free.

RICK. Settle down.

SETH. Thank you.

JENNY. I'm serious. Xu Wei won't care if someone paints anti-capitalist graffiti outside his door. I mean yes, if he's in our fund, maybe you won't be invited to like, the MoMA Benefit this year but you hate modern art anyway.

RICK. I really do, but Katie likes it.

JENNY. We can do whatever we want if he's in, which means actually we have to go with my plan.

SETH. Your plan is fucking insane and no one likes it. How many times do we have to repeat things to you?

JENNY. Our fundamental concerns have changed. Try to keep up.

RICK. We'll scare off future LPs.

JENNY. Then we'll tap Xu Wei's network.

SETH. No, no, stand back and look at what she's describing: an American business, aggressively downsized, and then the value of that business is actually sucked out of the US economy and sent overseas, to a guy who made his money selling / repurposed nuclear material

JENNY. / To be fair, that's never been proven.

SETH. All I'm saying is, you put yourself in the shoes of a regular guy, and I wonder, why should he have any faith in capitalism?

JENNY. Oh my gosh.

SETH. At some point, it starts to matter how people feel about you.

RICK. Could certainly kill our deal flow.

SETH. Not just that.

My first year at Yale, I dated this girl. I remember one night we were at a party and it came out that her dad was an executive at Philip Morris. And I remember she got so defensive, so fast. Before anyone even said anything, she started saying: 'You know, tobacco companies, despite what you might think, they really didn't know. They didn't know.' Well they fucking knew, right? Everyone knows they fucking knew.

RICK. Yeah.

SETH. I don't want that to be my kid, telling lies about me so she won't be embarrassed at Yale.

JENNY. Already settling for a second-tier Ivy. Probably for the best.

SETH. Your wedding is in what, six weeks?

RICK. Yeah.

SETH. A three-day party at your Bali estate. Let's say he does commit enough and we close on Landmark. Your wedding will happen during that period of time. How is Katie gonna feel if her wedding gets attacked in the papers?

RICK. My personal life cannot factor into this decision.

SETH. Of course. But we saw what happened with the engagement party. The things that got said about you guys. This is your wedding. I know it's easy to think that like, only people in laundry commercials enjoy their weddings. But honestly, my and Rebecca's wedding was one of the best days of my life. And you and Katie – at your Bali place, on the water, it's gonna be incredible.

RICK. Yeah.

SETH. I'm saying: let's make the right call here. And I'm not just talking about the effect on our lives. I'm talking about the future of this firm.

JENNY. If Xu Wei allocates with us, we will have a fiduciary responsibility to him to go for the highest possible return.

SETH (*ignoring her*). Show the world that we deserve at least a little bit of trust. Show *The Times* that they're wrong about you. You don't destroy jobs, you create jobs.

RICK. We've been treated unfairly.

SETH. That's right. Let's not confirm the bullshit that's being said about us.

JENNY (*doing a bit*). Oh, you know what? This is embarrassing. I'm actually supposed to be in a meeting at my private equity firm. / What we do is

RICK. / Stop talking.

JENNY. Rick –

RICK. I said enough. I've heard enough from you today.

SETH. Rick, I've been working on this deal for months now. I know that my plan could return as much as three-point-two. So she found that stripping it down and grabbing a three-point-five. So fucking what? Are we really going to gut this company and fire all these people for a three-tenths difference?

RICK. No. We're not. I should've listened to you from the beginning.

JENNY. He's manipulating you: talking about your wedding, about your feelings.

SETH. With all due respect, you do not have perspective on that issue. You are alone.

JENNY. I'm not alone. There's a hawk on my shoulder.

Lights.

5.

That evening.

The same hotel bar.

JEFF *drinks seltzer water out of a nice glass. He emails someone on his phone.*

SETH *enters.*

JEFF. Hey man.

SETH. There you are. How's it going?

JEFF. You gonna grab a drink?

SETH. No, I'm good. I read over that addendum on the way over.

JEFF. It doesn't commit you guys to anything.

SETH. It commits us to the goal of avoiding labor cuts.

JEFF. But there's nothing measureable.

SETH. Legal won't let us sign a binding agreement about our management plan / at this stage

JEFF. / Okay yeah, yeah I've heard that like ten times / today man

SETH. / And Jeff, hold on. I want you to understand something: The guarantee you're looking for – it's unnecessary. After you left, Rick confirmed, again, that he's going with our plan. Okay?

JEFF. Okay. But, I have to ask…

SETH. Please, ask me anything. I want you to be comfortable.

JEFF. Who's John Kim?

SETH. What?

JEFF. Does a dude named John Kim work for you guys?

SETH. Yeah, he's one of Jenny's analysts. Why?

JEFF. Dana's friend Lynn called me this morning. Lynn's a commercial broker at Collier's Real Estate. She said a guy named John Kim called her office twice yesterday evening. Real fast talker, she said she had to ask him to slow down.

SETH. Uh-huh.

JEFF. She said he asked about large-scale properties downtown, and he specifically asked what the price point would be if the Landmark building were available for lease.

SETH. That's so silly.

JEFF. We gave you the numbers on that property months ago.

SETH. I know, maybe he was vetting the numbers.

JEFF. It's a fucking weird way to vet the numbers.

SETH. That's Jenny, she makes her analysts triangulate.

JEFF. But why would it be framed that way?

SETH. Jeff I've been through lots of buyouts. I can tell you, honestly, you have no reason to be worried here.

JEFF. Last night sitting right here in this bar, you asked me how I'd feel if Rick departed from our plan.

SETH. That was just a question.

JEFF. Shit like that is never just a question.

SETH. In this case, it was. Look, I know this step can be scary. You've been at the controls because Stu has been effectively retired, vacationing with Julie all the damn time. This is normal.

JEFF. I want to be in business with you.

SETH. Me too. I think your questions are great – it shows you're serious, you can get granular. That's what makes you a great CEO.

JEFF. It just bothers me. Everything you and I mapped out, at no point did we talk about vacating that building.

SETH. Rick is gonna do what you and I want him to do.

JEFF. But the addendum doesn't obligate him to that.

SETH. Okay, you're right: he has the ultimate say. But he's on our side.

JEFF. Have other plans been discussed?

SETH. Nothing that's actually serious.

JEFF. But other plans have been discussed.

SETH. Yes, in hypothetical terms. That's Rick's MO.

JEFF. Were you going to tell me about that?

SETH. No, because it wasn't serious.

JEFF. I mean, obviously it's serious enough that this John guy called Collier's twice.

SETH. Rick's MO is: Let me look at an organization from every possible angle and ask every question I can think of: Do they need the jet? Do they need production in California? That kind of thing.

JEFF. He talked about offshoring.

SETH. I think he talked about nearshoring.

JEFF. We want production to stay in Sacramento.

SETH. And it will. Rick likes to do thought experiments. That's all.

JEFF. Can I see these thought experiments?

SETH. They aren't even fleshed-out business models. But if you want that information, I guess I can try to get an analyst to write something up for you.

JEFF. No, no, that's fine.

SETH. Are you sure?

JEFF. Yeah.

SETH. Alright.

JEFF. Since we're talking about hypotheticals…

Let's say I don't sign the LOI. Landmark walks away from the table, no buyout.

SETH. Jeff, it's going to be / fine

JEFF. / Hear me out. It's a thought experiment. The fact is: We have the brand, we have the new designs, we have a detailed plan. Hypothetically speaking, why don't we just fucking do it on our own?

SETH. What?

JEFF. I could hire you.

SETH. What?

JEFF. Right now Landmark doesn't have anyone who possesses even a fraction of your skills or your contacts. If I hired you, you could find us capital from another source, we could cash Stu out, and we could do our plan without your firm. Six years from now, we could be coming back here with our huge IPO.

SETH. The whole plan is to do that after the buyout.

JEFF. I know. But did a private equity firm tell Apple to go from computers to iPhones? No. They did it on their own.

SETH. That's a very specific case.

JEFF. And I hope you won't take this the wrong way, but: Working on Wall Street, don't you feel like that's lost its prestige a little bit?

SETH. I work in Midtown.

JEFF. You know what I mean.

SETH. I don't, actually.

JEFF. Look at this past week. Look what people are saying about your firm. Don't you worry what the situation will look like for you guys in ten years, twenty years?

SETH. I'll be running my own firm in ten years.

JEFF. My point is, when people ask you what you do for a living, how do you feel about your answer?

SETH. Well. That's quite a thing to say.

JEFF. I didn't mean any / disrespect

SETH. / Our buyout is the instrument that will allow you to get the salary you deserve and free you up to run Landmark the way you want. Or do you want things to stay as they are?

JEFF. Of course not. It was just a hypothetical. Rick has his thought experiments. I have mine.

SETH. If you're saying you want to walk away at this point, then I can call Rick and we can have that conversation.

JEFF. I'm not saying that. I'm not saying that at all. And I meant no disrespect.

SETH. None taken.

JEFF. Look, I wasn't expressing myself well. My point is: I think you're one of those guys who makes everyone around him better. You have vision, you can see what's coming, ten steps ahead. Not everyone has that. You're the number-one reason I've been so excited about this buyout. Of course I want to do it, alright?

SETH. Okay.

JEFF. Okay.

SETH. I'm sorry that analyst was making calls. I'll bring that up with Jenny.

JEFF. It's not a big thing.

SETH. No, I'm glad you brought it up. You have any other concerns, any at all, you come to me.

JEFF. Thanks man.

SETH. You know what? You relax, get a good night's sleep. I'll tell Rick you need another day or so before you're ready to sign.

JEFF. I do want to pull the trigger on this. We want this deal, we need it.

SETH. We can do it first thing Monday. That'll give you the weekend to think through every other question or concern you might have, and you know me, I'm around, we can talk it out.

JEFF. Okay.

SETH. Hey. It's all happening.

JEFF. Yeah man. It's all happening.

Lights.

6.

Saturday.

SETH *and* JENNY *wait outside a room in Hong Kong.*

SETH *has a tack in his hair but doesn't know that.*

They sit in silence for a bit. Eventually JENNY *turns to him.*

JENNY. If I were sitting in a town car,

in traffic,

and like let's say I'd answered all my emails,

and the markets weren't open yet,

so to pass the time I checked the news,

and I saw a headline saying a Manhattan man was hit by a bus and his body parts went flying everywhere,

I would think to myself: Oh my gosh, I hope it was Seth.

SETH. I might retire young.

So by sixty, I'll be living in Portofino with Rebecca.

I'll stare out at the ocean, and I'll think over my life. And I'll be happy, and I'll be proud. Maybe one day, for one unpleasant second, my thoughts will land on you.

And if I start to wonder what you're up to, I'll realize: There's no question.

You'll be in New York.

Still at it.

Still trying to squeeze every single dollar out of someone else's deal.

But Jenny, the sad thing is, at some point, people will stop listening to you.

Because you'll never run your own firm. You'll be an old woman who's never actually been in charge of anything.

JENNY. So what age, exactly, do you plan to retire?

SETH. That's not the point.

JENNY. I'd like to set an alert on my phone.

Silence. They wait.

How much do you think it'll be?

SETH. What?

JENNY. Xu Wei's allocation.

SETH. No idea.

JENNY. Fifty-five? I know he wanted to give us fifty-five recently. Until Rick insulted him…

SETH. And there's our great buzz right now.

JENNY. Yeah a denaturalized Chinese gangster is really concerned about ex-ShopGreat cashiers who now have to work at the CVS twenty yards away in the same strip mall.

SETH. Shh. Someone could hear you.

And he's not a gangster.

JENNY. Rick's said that in the past.

SETH. Seriously someone could hear you.

I hate waiting.

JENNY. Me too.

SETH. I thought leaving Goldman meant less of this.

JENNY. There has been less of it.

Silence. They wait.

SETH. Did you see that fish tank downstairs?

JENNY. Oh yeah.

SETH. Fucking creepy.

JENNY. Shh, someone could hear you.

Silence. They wait.

Is it a boy or girl?

SETH. It's a girl. Don't you remember all the It's A Girl balloons and crap people put in my office?

JENNY. I thought that was talking about you.

SETH. Cute.

JENNY. No I really did.

SETH. No that's really funny.

Silence. They wait.

What if he only wants to give fifty-five and he won't go higher? Then we're tied to him and we still can't buy Landmark.

JENNY. Yeah. And we wouldn't be able to do the Amalgamated Syringe deal either. Humiliating. Like arriving for an important meeting in a yellow cab.

SETH. What's wrong with yellow cabs?

JENNY. I got stuck on the FDR with a cabbie who launched into the detailed story of his escape from Uganda in the 1970s. It was torture. Ever since that day, I only do towncars.

SETH. I always like hearing cab driver's stories.

JENNY. Of course you do. You probably ask for them.

Silence. They wait.

There's a thumb tack in your hair.

SETH. What?

JENNY. There's a thumb tack in your hair. It's been there for hours.

SETH. Where is it? Why didn't you tell me?

JENNY. No don't touch it you might push it into your scalp.

SETH. Why didn't you tell me?

She removes it.

JENNY. I put it there when you were asleep on the plane.

SETH. What the fuck?

JENNY. It was a long flight. I was bored.

SETH. It could have damaged my head.

JENNY. And what a loss that would have been.

SETH. What the fuck Jenny.

Silence. They wait.

JENNY. Gosh it's taking a long time.

SETH. He'll say yes.

JENNY. This is really taking forever.

Eventually, RICK *comes out.*

Is he in?

RICK. He's in.

JENNY. How much?

RICK. Three hundred.

SETH. What?

JENNY. Three hundred?

He nods.

SETH. Holy shit.

RICK. We're back.

JENNY. The fund's at three-one-nine now. That's three-one-nine.

SETH. He's committing three hundred?

RICK. He has excessive cash and few places to put it.

SETH. Right.

RICK. I'm telling the bank.

(*To* SETH.) We need the CEO to sign the fucking LOI. Is he still in New York?

SETH. Yeah.

RICK. Can you set a meeting with us and him?

SETH. I can handle the LOI, don't worry about it.

RICK. No, I want to be there.

SETH. Okay. Why?

RICK. I wanna do this right.

JENNY. What does that mean?

RICK *places a call.*

RICK. I want to offer him a bonus.

(*On the phone.*) Michael it's locked down, we're back up to three-one-nine. So that'll be what, after Landmark?

JENNY. Two-twenty-point-eight.

RICK (*on the phone*). Two-twenty-point-eight million in dry powder. Get me the memo on that syringe company. I want something to read during my massage.

RICK *hangs up.*

SETH. Why are we offering him a bonus?

RICK. What?

SETH. Why are we offering Jeff a bonus? We can just increase his salary if we're doing the growth play.

RICK. Oh. I decided to go with her plan.

SETH. We agreed that was the wrong move.

RICK. I changed my mind.

SETH. We need the good press.

RICK. Not when he's in for three hundred.

SETH. Okay, but we can't push through a huge round of layoffs right before your wedding.

RICK. Her plan'll get us a higher return.

Can you wait for his lawyer? He'll have copies of the agreement.

JENNY. Okay.

RICK. See you both at dinner.

RICK *leaves*.

JENNY. I love Hong Kong.

SETH. Why doesn't he listen to me?

JENNY. It's a great world city.

SETH. He'll regret this. When Katie leaves his ass because everyone is making fun of her wedding, he'll regret this.

JENNY. Conjecture: You are projecting your emotions onto Rick's fiancée.

SETH. Jeff is gonna lose his shit.

JENNY. Jeff works for us now.

SETH. He hasn't signed the LOI.

JENNY. He will.

SETH. And if he doesn't?

JENNY. If Jeff signs and stays on, he'll get a bonus.

SETH. He cares about Landmark, he cares about his employees.

JENNY. He probably also cares about getting a lot of money.

SETH. You don't know him. I fucking hope he doesn't sign it.

JENNY. If you sabotage this deal, Rick will know.

SETH. I don't care.

JENNY. He could fire you.

SETH. I don't care. If he doesn't sign, Rick will see how idiotic this is.

He thought the media was being unfair about his stupid elephants. Do you realize what people will think of us now?

JENNY. There are people who think we're part of a global conspiracy to enslave ninety-nine percent of the world population. There are people who think Goldman runs a shadow government. Allow less intelligent people to hate you. It's their destiny and it costs you nothing.

SETH. It'll cost us everything.

JENNY. Okay, I was trying to help you feel better.

SETH. And I wanted to grow this company. To create jobs, not massive layoffs.

JENNY. They'll get hired somewhere else.

SETH. And if they can't?

JENNY. If you don't acquire the training to secure income for yourself, then you're going to have a rocky time. This has always been the case.

SETH. Fifteen years ago, I was so proud to get picked by Goldman.

JENNY. Me too.

SETH. And now, everyone hates us.

JENNY. No, it's jealousy.

SETH. It's hatred. I don't care what we'll make this year. It's not worth it.

JENNY. Okay. Then leave. Start an organic farm.

SETH. I'm being serious.

JENNY. No, you're being unserious.

SETH. Rick would have been perfectly happy with the return on my plan, and you had to ruin everything.

JENNY. Your plan was an expensive attempt to prop up an outdated company.

SETH. Alright Jenny. You're being fucking dumb, or you're being dishonest. It's one of the two.

JENNY. Landmark is more valuable with its unnecessary assets and expenses stripped away so it can be flipped in this market. That is a conclusion drawn from facts.

SETH. It's not more valuable. Not to me. Not to Jeff. Not to the people who work there.

JENNY. Okay. Spare me the *Frontline* episode please.

SETH. You can act like this is simple, but it's not simple. There will be a real cost to this bullshit. I think on some level you know that, and you refuse to face it.

JENNY. You're saying that I'm dishonest.

SETH. That's right.

JENNY. That's funny Seth.

SETH. Is it?

JENNY. Yeah because I think, that of the two of us, I am not the deceptive one.

Lights.

7.

Monday.

KMM Capital Management. Midtown Manhattan.

JEFF *and* SETH.

JEFF *finishes reading a document.* SETH *takes it.*

SETH. I know.

JEFF. Bangladesh?

SETH. Yeah.

JEFF. Is this serious?

SETH. There was a shift in thinking.

JEFF. What shift?

SETH. Nothing to do with Landmark.

JEFF. Just looking at that, with those changes, you can forget about growth. We might not even maintain stable sales.

SETH. Yeah. That's why I wanted you to know. I told him this is a mistake. He doesn't listen. He does not fucking listen. Man I'm so sorry, I've been so angry about this situation.

JEFF. Seth.

SETH. They're gonna be here in a second. You can tell Rick the deal is dead, and you can walk the fuck out of here. Put it on me if you want.

JEFF. Okay but / Seth, we

SETH. / Another firm can do the buyout. I'll give you some names.

JEFF. But then what's gonna happen to you?

SETH. Don't worry about me.

JEFF. I can call Barb right now and have her start on the paperwork. Come work for Landmark.

SETH. Stu needs to be cashed out.

JEFF. Yeah, and I bet you can connect us with private investors. I can't raise that amount on my own, I don't have the access. I know I'd be lucky to have you.

SETH. You need to focus. They're gonna be here soon.

JEFF. Seth, I don't have a lot of options at this point.

SETH. That's not true.

JEFF. I get it if you need time to think.

SETH. This isn't about me right now.

JEFF. I disagree. This is about you. You know where the world's top business talent goes now? California. New York is done. You'd be out there, where innovation is actually happening. You'd be my partner – working every day with people who rely on you, sitting in on design meetings, putting your hands on an actual product you helped create. You'd be a real businessman.

SETH. I am a businessman.

JEFF. No you work in finance.

SETH. You say that like you believe the shit they wrote in *The Times*.

JEFF. No I say that because Stu and I agreed on four-nine-one because we thought you guys were being straightforward about what the business model would be, and now we're getting the bait-and-switch.

SETH. It wasn't a bait-and-switch. I fought for our plan.

JEFF. Okay and they ignored you. And look, I know you make a fucking ton of money here, but in a few years when everyone in America has one of our pieces and we go public, we could both end up with eight, maybe nine figures.

SETH. That's not a sure thing.

JEFF. It's as close to a sure thing as I've seen, my whole career.

SETH. No business plan is a sure thing.

JEFF. You were pretty confident about it when it was gonna be done through your firm.

SETH. Yeah, that was different.

JEFF. How?

SETH. It's different. You understand.

JEFF. Why is it different?

RICK *and* JENNY *enter.*

RICK. Jeff. There you are.

JENNY. Welcome back.

JEFF. Hi.

JENNY. So, we're ready to initiate close, which means we need you to finally sign this thing.

SETH. Rick, we have a problem.

RICK. What's up?

SETH. Last week, Jenny's analysts were calling all around Sacramento asking some very targeted questions. That got back to Jeff, and now he's struggling with the idea that our buyout could mean a different direction for Landmark.

RICK. I see.

JENNY. Seth.

SETH. We know my growth play is what made us an attractive buyout partner for Jeff and Stu. So now we have a problem.

RICK (*to* JEFF). At this point, we need to move forward on the deal or we need to move on.

JEFF. I understand.

RICK. It's up to you. Deals die all the time. I will say, it's rare for a CEO to kill it in this situation.

JEFF. I have to do what's best for Landmark.

RICK. Let's be clear. You're gonna keep your job.

JEFF. I know.

RICK. And I'd like to offer you a bonus.

SETH. I don't think there's a number you can put in front of him that will make this okay.

RICK. Then Jeff can give us a number.

JENNY. You'd get half today, half when we exit the investment. And this would be on top of the salary increase we'll negotiate after close.

RICK. I'll be transparent. We want this to happen, and we want you there.

Excited to take this journey with you.

RICK *goes*.

JENNY. I'd like to tell you two things –

SETH. Jenny –

JENNY. One, you're the CEO, you'll be a part of any decision we make with regard to operational changes. Now, it's obvious that Seth has told you we won't be getting into the bespoke-luggage business. Starting a whole dialogue about that would be an inefficient use of time.

JEFF. I agree.

JENNY. Two, and I apologize for being straightforward if that's not your style, but Landmark is undergoing a process of decay. You know this. That's why you were so enthusiastic about changing it. Soon, no one will buy Landmark. Especially if they know we walked away after doing our diligence. This is almost certainly the best offer you'll get.

SETH. She has no way of knowing that for sure.

JENNY. Okay, I'm getting Rick back in here.

JEFF. No, it's fine. Please just give me a moment.

SETH. You can walk away from this deal. Another firm will do the buyout.

JENNY. He's right. They will. But if you run to a desperate deal-starved firm in a panic tomorrow morning, there will be no bonus attached to that transaction –

SETH. Jenny –

JENNY. And in the end, they'd put Landmark through similar cuts.

SETH. The thing you'll never / understand

JEFF. / What kind of number would he do, for the bonus?

SETH. What?

JENNY. Aim high, we'll tell you if we can't do it.

SETH. Are you seriously considering this?

JEFF. What would happen to my people? Can you tell me that to my face?

JENNY. Sure. Most of them will need to find new jobs.

SETH. And there it is.

JENNY. Jeff, I don't know what has gone on between you and Seth, and I don't care because it doesn't matter. I can say this: I may not end up being your best friend, but I will not deceive you.

JEFF. Yeah.

SETH. Don't do this. You can walk away.

JEFF. If you won't come to Landmark to execute the exact plan we've been talking about for months, then it's pretty fucking obvious you never believed in this idea in the first place.

SETH. Of course I did.

JEFF. Then come to California with me.

JENNY. Oh my gosh.

JEFF. But you won't do that. Because then you'd have to take an actual risk.

JEFF writes down a number.

SETH. Holy shit.

She reads it. She's pleased.

JENNY. Interesting.

JEFF. What the hell does that mean?

She writes down a counter-offer.

JENNY. How about this?

JEFF. Do you have to check with Rick?

JENNY. Rick will do this.

JEFF. Jesus.

JENNY. Does that mean yes?

JEFF. I want seventy percent now, thirty when you exit.

JENNY. Sixty-five, thirty-five. But we need an answer.

JEFF. Will Rick do sixty-five percent up-front?

JENNY. Yes.

JEFF. Okay. Okay.

SETH. What about Stu? This is a business he built from nothing.

JEFF. Stu's seventy-nine. He's in Cabo with Julie. He doesn't care at this point.

SETH. Right. I see who you are now.

JEFF. Excuse me?

SETH. I was really excited to work together, but now I see…

JEFF. You see what?

SETH. You said 'layoffs are brutal,' you said 'I care about my employees.' But the only thing you actually care about is how much money you can squeeze of us to pay for your failing winery.

JENNY. Oh my gosh Seth.

JEFF *signs the Letter of Intent.*

JEFF. Landmark needs the capital. Stu needs to be bought out. But yeah, I need the money. I need it for my mortgage, and I need it for the winery. Maybe that makes me selfish. See look at that, I told the truth. See how easy that is?

SETH. When have I lied?

JEFF (*to* JENNY). Are we done here?

JENNY. We'll be in touch tomorrow.

JEFF. Alright.

SETH. No I want you to tell me, when have I lied?

JEFF *goes.*

JENNY. Wow. That got really uncomfortable. Do you want to talk about it?

SETH. No.

JENNY. I can't believe you actually did that. And for what?

People like that – They blame us, they take our money. They blame us, they take our money.

RICK *returns.*

RICK (*to* JENNY). We good?

The Amalgamated Syringe guys are getting impatient.

JENNY. Yes, I'll get started. Here's what Schrader wants.

It's an easy number.

RICK. Great.

JENNY. I know.

She goes.

RICK. Were you trying to throw a grenade at this?

SETH. I should've known the bonus would work. He's cash poor.

RICK. Yeah. Not anymore.

SETH. There are two young analysts I really like. Jamil and David. I want to take them with me, if that's alright.

RICK. Where do you think you're going?

Seth, I'm not gonna fire you.

SETH. Okay.

RICK. This was huge, you brought it to us at just the right time. Show people we aren't gonna sit in the shadows when we're taking fire.

You see that piece in the *Journal*?

SETH. No.

RICK. New PR gal's really upset. Never thought I'd see the day, the *Journal* coming at me like that.

SETH. Oh.

RICK. Don't worry about it. Xu Wei doesn't care.

SETH. What about Katie?

RICK. Oh she's fine. She and some girlfriends went to Provence for the week.

SETH. Ah.

RICK. I want you to know, you're a real asset. Even when you're a pain in my ass. But deals like this could not happen without you. I'm well aware of that.

SETH. What'd they say in the *Journal*?

RICK. What?

SETH. The *Journal* thing. What'd they say about you?

RICK. It was stupid. And tomorrow my foundation is announcing the new school we're building in Bali. That'll help with all this.

SETH. Yeah.

RICK. At the end of the day – it's your name on a building that lasts.

SETH. Right.

RICK. Katie gets so upset about people being hard on us, and I tell her: Honey, look at my foundation, look at the school we're building for the little Balinese kids. That's what people will remember about me.

SETH. Then they'll have it wrong.

RICK. What?

SETH. They'll have it wrong.

Lights.

8.

One week later.

JENNY *speaks at NYU.*

JENNY. Hi guys. So nice to see your shining faces.

I'll be honest, I had a hard time determining what to talk about today.

I actually spoke with Rick about it. And he said just talk about your life, tell a little story to show who you are. Which: Of course. I should have seen that myself. I've learned a lot from Rick. Mentors.

I don't know how instructive my experiences are because I'm atypical and I didn't go to NYU, but the recent hysterical whining directed at my firm has caused me to reflect on something that happened to me in high school:

I took AP calculus in 10th grade, and my school didn't offer any math higher than that so in 11th grade I had to go to the local community college to take multivariable calculus.

Unfortunately, my family forced me to ride to the community college with a girl who was a full-time student there. This was Lindsay, our neighbor's daughter.

Lindsay was twenty, and she had still not been able to pass Algebra One.

As you might imagine, we had little in common. And she was rude to me. When I would request that she obey the speed limit, she would actually exert more force on the accelerator. I knew what was going on. What was going on had a name: Resentment.

So finally one morning I turned to Lindsay and I said: You aren't failing Algebra One because I'm acing multivariable calculus. Those are independent events.

Let me repeat that, because that's something you need to keep in mind when people attack you because you work in finance:

There will always be people who fail Algebra One. But those people did not fail Algebra One because you were able to ace multivariable calculus. We are simply in a different class. And to that we could perhaps attach some meaning but that meaning is not that you and I are the villains of the story.

I said to Lindsay: All I can possibly do is continue my progress through multivariable calculus and try not to spill my juice in your car, and maybe you can please drive safely. That's the most we can do for each other.

Anyway, she became very angry.

She said how dare I bring that up. She said she wanted to be a lawyer some day (of course) and she was never going to get there because she can't do math.

So I said what do you mean you can't do math?

I asked to see her homework. She was stuck in the middle of the first equation. There was a fraction she couldn't simplify.

I still remember it was x to the seventh power over x squared.

That's the operation she couldn't complete: x to the seventh power over x squared.

So I said, since it's the same base, you can just subtract the exponents. We have x to the seventh in the numerator and x squared in the denominator, so now we have x to the fifth.

Simplified.

But she didn't get it.

I was like, Lindsay this is simple subtraction.

That was an anecdote from my life.

I'm going to finish nine and a half minutes early because I have nothing else to say and I don't believe in wasting time.

That's all I have.

End of Play.